YOUR PASSPORT TO BUSINESS LEADERSHIP

Awareness   **Solution**   **Connection**

"All invention begins as a thought"
TMC

Dedicated to:
Thomas Corry 1V

*"He lived his life in radiance
and gave his heart to everyone."*

Editor: Johanna Chase

PRODUCED BY LONGRUN PRESS email: t2516413@yahoo.com

Table of Contents

FOR THOSE WHO TRULY LOVE THEIR BUSINESS

Introduction

PROFIT offers advantages over most business books in strategy and thought organization. Multiplied awareness and accurate perception are taught through the following strategies.

PROFIT teaches:

Solving problems
Defeating emotional conflicts
Developing warrior skills

PROFIT magnifies the power of your talents by harnessing the intellectual, emotional and strategic discipline you need to keep your mind alert and fosters accurate business thinking.

The surprising secrets of business survival are unveiled. PROFIT melds thinking, emotion, mystical into a focused business force. This gives rise to multiplied awareness and accurate perception.

Multiplied awareness is the internal light that powers your enterprise and leads to excellence. Accurate perception leads to correct thinking and appropriate business actions.

Essence of PROFIT

The purpose of PROFIT is to make your vision of a business a reality. This book takes you step by step through the business creation process and magnifies the power of your talents. PROFIT harnesses the intellectual, emotional and strategic discipline you need to keep your mind alert and fosters accurate business thinking.

PROFIT discipline allows you to gain awareness on different levels. We call this "the power of multiplied awareness." With this skill, you can control events and enjoy the sweet satisfaction of business success. Your perception excels.

In the boiling pot of human activity, businesses can take whatever form humans create to meet the challenges of survival. PROFIT teaches the fundamental principles that apply to ALL businesses -- no matter what their nature. And encourages a scientific approach to business creation.

PROFIT addresses business survival essentials:

Needed– an organized thinking process if your business is to survive a fast changing world.

Needed– multiplied awareness to help insure accurate perception. If perception is wrong-your resources can be squandered and business survival chances diminished.

Building a business begins when you become aware of a commercial need. You then create a product or service to solve that need. You define a market. And begin selling the product. You have created an economic engine.

Three Pillars of Business Success

PROFIT proposes a business built on three constructs:

- Awareness
- Solution
- Connection.

They are called the three pillars of success. By using the pillars you can check the health of the business. In the process of checking, the gift called multiplied awareness develops.The process allows your mind to stay on high alert

The three pillars of business success help to insure business stability. The pillars mental model is a convenient way to visualize the progress of your business start-up. It enhances fact based thinking.

The power of multiplied awareness helps you to develop an accurate perception of what is happening. Accuracy in allocation of resources and actions is the result. Strengthening the survival power of your enterprise.

As your business matures, the model provides a way to check economic health. As you create your enterprise, your mind integrates all the pillars of success into your business dynamic. And improves your comprehension.

The power of multiplied awareness helps you to develop an accurate perception of what is happening. And leads to a well thought out allocation of resources and actions. You strengthen business sustenance and surviving powers.

Under the PROFIT Method, the three pillars model allows your business mind to stay on high alert.

PROFIT introduces you to psychological tools that prevent basic human emotions from sabotaging you and holding you back from having a successful business.

The PROFIT Method also teaches an effective approach to winning: it combines your thoughts, emotions and fighting ability into a unified force – turning you into a business warrior.

Realize Your Destiny

The pillars of Awareness, Solution and Connection all exist in unison in your business. Each pillar requires you to expand your awareness. Business, emotion, and strategy also multiply awareness.

When you combine this concept with a reality that grows from your vision, your business idea is built on a solid foundation.

The PROFIT Method of business design brings awareness into existence, turns challenges into solutions, and transforms ideas into action by creating connections.

Smart business is defined by:

- Marketing **Awareness**
- Smart **Solutions**
- Creating **Connections.**

These combined components of commerce create the three pillars of business success.

Transforming Emotional Energy

You need to harness latent energy to be successful in a new business.

People in business endure three emotional distresses: rejection, anger and fear.

Successful entrepreneurs transform the energies locked in these emotions into tools for success, so that they become valuable assets.

- Rejection sharpens awareness.
- Fear broadens vision.
- Anger unblocks creativity.

If you are in pain due to fear, rejection or anger, you trap your vital energies in rocky emotional canyons.
Unblocking these canyons frees the energy flow, so you can achieve your goals.

Harness this energy. Get on top of anger and tap into the creative impulses of your mind. Discover alternatives.

Win the battle and become a business warrior by:

- Turning off your inner dialogue.
- Having no expectations.
- Taking responsibility.
- Being a warrior.

The timeline of an idea begins when visualization kicks in -- and ends when awareness leads to substance.

The Way of the Warrior

(Adapted from the writings of Carlos Castaneda)

- Turn off your inner dialogue.
- Have no expectations.
- Take responsibility.
- Be a warrior.

"The basic difference between an ordinary man and a warrior is that a warrior takes everything as a challenge while an ordinary man takes everything as a blessing or a curse."

"Only as a warrior can one withstand the path of knowledge. A warrior cannot complain or regret anything. His life is an endless challenge, and challenges cannot possibly be good or bad. Challenges are simply challenges."

"The warrior aims to be impeccable in whatever he does, but never takes himself and his actions too seriously, considering them as controlled folly. He acts with sustained effort and unbending intent in order to raise his level of energy."

"A man of knowledge lives by acting, not by thinking about acting. "

"All of us, whether or not we are warriors, have a cubic centimeter of chance that pops out in front of our eyes from time to time. The difference between an average man and a warrior is that the warrior is aware of this, and one of his tasks is to be alert, deliberately waiting, so that when his cubic centimeter pops out he has the necessary speed, the prowess, to pick it up."

PROFIT helps develop understanding and awareness of how to construct the foundation of your business.

This nurturing, focused approach allows you to access, refine, and fortify the keystone of any business to withstand the tremors of today's markets.

The *Gallery of Innovation,* featured later in the book, showcases successful businesses. Illustrating WHAT to sell, these featured businesses are graded on how well they use the Three Pillars approach.

Awakening Business Consciousness

The PROFIT Method gives a clear picture of the structural realities of business. It helps you create desired results for your business, through the power of multiplied awareness.

The PROFIT Method

- Provides a way to understand business.
- Defines the basic concepts that make business an integral part of a functioning society.
- Shows the relationships between people, products, buying, and selling – and what makes a business viable.
- Illuminates the stark realities of why businesses fail.
- Offers tools and guidance to help you succeed in your business venture with unerring perception.

The PROFIT Method also presents two sets of psychological tools: One set is for the inner world and the other set -- taught by Carlos Castaneda* -- is for the outer world.

The tools help you gear up your psyche to overcome obstacles threatening the survival of your enterprise. The Three Pillars model combines these psychological tools -- forming an efficient approach to growing and managing a profitable business.

Definition
Business: the practice of making a living by buying and selling.

Reasons to Start a Business

There are many reasons to start a business. Some of the most common are:

- Economic survival
- Inner motivation
- Escaping a "dead-end" job
- An idea, concept or product with commercial value
- Personal fulfillment
- A need for adventure
- Intuition

Your reason is the keystone of your success. Your progress requires you to unfold important parallel efforts defined by the Three Pillars of Business Success:

- Awareness
- Solution
- Connection

In the context of the reason, your management needs to be guided by long-term goals. It helps to rethink the entire business model while considering:

- the motivation of your staff
- how you use your assets
- the changes you need to make to progress toward profitable growth. Fact based intelligence required.

Fashioning a New Business

A new business -- with a focused foundation -- meets a need.

Creating a new business means bringing your ideas into reality. Giving your ideas form, mass and functionality.

Examples:

- Developing new computer software programs and systems information
- In writing or music, when you create new combinations of words or sounds -- or even a genre -- that does not yet exist. When you finish the "doing" process, the words become readable and the sounds enter our ears. You validate your reverie.

The three pillars of Awareness, Solution and Connection give strength and direction to your creation. They reinforce what you think and implement.

Visualization helps create an idea, product, or service. This critical essence of creativity allows awareness to emerge into reality, by bringing your vision into existence.

When you redirect your energy, you can deal with unexpected obstacles. You become passionate about your creation, and can apply the full force of your intellect to protect and sustain its progress.

"Every adversity has the seed of an equivalent or greater benefit."
Napoleon Hill

When you perceive your whole business as greater than the sum of its parts, you create an economic machine. You make sense of the whole – you don't only see the individual parts. You see how the parts connect. You think clearly.

The PROFIT model helps assess prospects for your business by using multiplied awareness.

Multiplied Awareness

Multiplied awareness allowed an almost bankrupt Apple Computer to transform itself into the successful corporation it is today.

When the Apollo 13 crew and Houston were struggling to avert disaster, the crew used multiplied awareness to overcome several life-threatening system failures and return safely to earth. The feat required unerring thinking.

Sharpen your business skills and enjoy prosperity with PROFIT, by:

- Harnessing the power of multiplied awareness.
- Building on the three pillars of Business Success.
- Transforming emotional energy.
- Becoming a warrior.

These actions create powerful business entities. And give you the competence for superior enterprise design.

.

Accurate Perception

Accurate perception is built upon the foundation provided by the three pillars, emotion transformation, warrior skills and multiplied awareness. These elements help to build a mental image upon which decisions are made.

The brain enables individuals to see the world around them as stable, even though the input information may be incomplete and rapidly varying. Therefore it is important to continually update your information elements to insure accurate perception.

Example: perception checks:

Are you looking through a keyhole or getting the big picture?

Are you checking emotions- are fear or anger dominating your judgment?

Are you completely aware of all the parameters in play?

Are the three pillars functioning correctly?

Your conscious awareness helps insure accurate perception and your realization of business reality.

Review

Starting a profitable business requires three disciplines: structural, emotional and strategic.

Multiplied awareness enhances management.

Accurate perception helps in allocating resources.

Begin with the dream -- the vision of your business. Create reality by building your three pillars : Awareness, Solution, and Connection. Allow unerring perception and accurate thinking to guide your progress.

By breathing life into the unknown future, your mind mines possibilities and supplies intuitive solutions. Your critical thinking and vision align, inviting destiny to guide your vision toward reality. Creative discipline brings your vision into reality.

Awareness

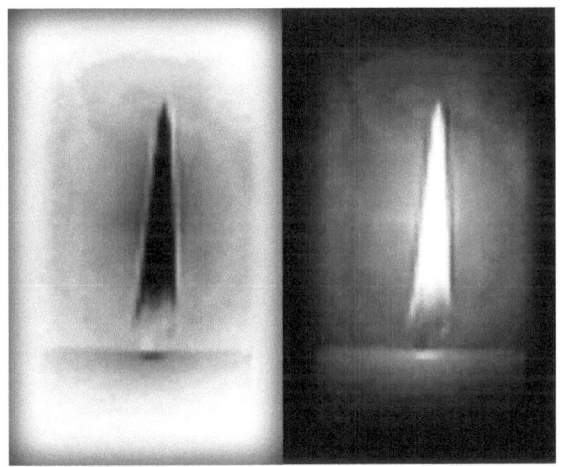

*"A good idea is worth just
as much as anything in this
world, and people want it
just as badly".*

Ben Corry

Awareness

Cultivating awareness depends on how you:

- Perceive what is going on -- how things fit together, which ideas work or don't work, creating mental solutions, and discovering answers.

- Recognize all elements that influence and constrain the flow of events in a transaction, in solving a problem, and/or determining a course of action.

- Recognize elements that make up a product, a system, and/or course of action.

- Write down/record ideas for future action.

The Change Factor: nature's love of metamorphosis

Most business models, out of necessity, are based in a fixed universe. However, every aspect of the model's conceptual framework changes over time. Some parts of the model never seem to change. Other parts change overnight.

The challenge you face is that you bang your head against a wall of assumptions you believe are correct - rather than changing your assumptions to fit reality. This is difficult, yet necessary.

The most successful enterprises develop the awareness to be flexible in planning – to remain in sync with the realities of the moment. They encourage fact based thinking. Accurate perception is essential for efficient management.

1. If you're not aware of what is happening, you fail.
2. If you can't solve the problem, you fail.
3. If you can't make the connection, you fail.

This may sound harsh, but there is no way to escape the consequences of failed actions. You must be aware of the Three Pillars- their consequences and benefits.

Completing all three activities invites total success.

This book teaches the concept of multiplied awareness – this means simultaneous awareness at all three levels in the business management process.

1. Be aware of the Pillars of Success.
2. Be aware of your internal emotional state.
3. Be aware of the way of the warrior.

These are the core teachings of PROFIT.

Multiple awareness is the skill that lifts your business to the highest levels of profitability and sustainability.

Quotes

"Awareness without action is worthless.
Dr. Phil McGraw

"Impossible only means that you haven't found the solution yet.
Anonymous

"It's easy to come up with new ideas; the hard part is letting go of what worked for you two years ago, but will soon be out of date."
Roger von Oech

"The best way to have a good idea is to have a lot of ideas."
Dr. Linus Pauling

"To raise new questions, new possibilities, to regard old problems from a new angle, requires creative imagination and marks real advance in science."
Albert Einstein

"Without playing with fantasy no creative work has ever yet come to birth. The debt we owe to the play of imagination is incalculable."
Carl Jung

"Once we rid ourselves of traditional thinking we can get on with creating the future."
James Bertrand

"Capital isn't so important in business. Experience isn't so important. You can get both these things. What is important is ideas. If you have ideas, you have the main asset you need, and there isn't any limit to what you can do with your business and your life."
Harvey Firestone

"The essential part of creativity is not being afraid to fail."
Edwin H. Land

"Creative activity could be described as a type of learning process where teacher and pupil are located in the same individual."
Arthur Koestler

"There is no doubt that creativity is the most important human resource of all. Without creativity, there would be no progress, and we would be forever repeating the same patterns."
Edward de Bono

"Great is the human who has not lost his childlike heart."
Mencius (Meng-Tse), 4th century BC

Solution

"Don't worry about people stealing your ideas. If your ideas are any good, you'll have to ram them down people's throats."
Howard Aiken

Is it time to bring your idea into reality?
If the answer is YES -- get started.

Open the door

Repeat out loud three times–
"I (say your name) will brave the unknown and persist in following my bliss."

Get on the road

1. Define the problem.
2. Plan the attack.
3. Work the plan.

Check if there's a solution on the horizon.

Course of action

Write down your wish. Keep it in your subconscious -- where it can work in the background of your thoughts. Know your strengths so you can build on them -- and use them to your advantage.

- See what others fail to see.
- Build your solution with accomplishments as building blocks.
- Use fear as an ally.
- Be persistent.

As you nurture your creativity and birth your idea, PROFIT encourages discipline and method.

Solution means finding a product or service that solves a problem. The solution is the core of your company. A product people want to buy can make you wealthy. Does your product solve a problem of economic value? If yes, plant the seed and help it grow.

Progressing from thought to invention is like stumbling around the house looking for a flashlight or a candle during a power outage.

Moving from thought to the reality of the invention means visiting the areas of consciousness from which human creativity emerges. Insights must be carefully harvested.

Productivity

Productivity is the heart and soul of a successful company.

To achieve maximum productivity, you have to set goals and establish priorities.

Setting goals increases productivity. It reduces false starts and forces you to think about what has to be done to reach your goals.

Setting long-term goals forces you to rethink what you are doing, how you motivate people, how you use your assets, and allows you to discover what you need to change to accomplish measurable jumps in profitable growth.

What goes on in an entrepreneur's head and heart? There are processes that differentiate an entrepreneur from the average breadwinner. Your body can feel the processes stimulating the brain.

There is more to starting a business than buying a book and following the steps. You need intestinal fortitude -- frustration and vision drive you. You feel the gut-wrenching problems as they appear – you tough it out and live the adventure. Give substance to your wishes. Create wealth. Survive.

Connection

"A dream you dream alone is only a dream.
A dream you dream together is reality."
John Lennon

Selling

What is selling? Selling is **handing over something in exchange for money.**

Saint Lucy of Syracuse is the patron of salespersons. Her name means "light." She walked her talk by demonstrating bravery and inner strength, qualities that are helpful to those who make their living selling.

Selling requires courage, foresight and integrity. Sales are essential for business success.

Selling is a basic human activity involving an alphabet of human mental strategies. Nothing happens in business until somebody buys something from someone.

*What Works In Sale***s**

- A product that sells itself.
- A sales person with thorough knowledge of the product and the ability to communicate the advantages to the consumer.
- Building goodwill.
- Knowledge of the customer's needs.
- Persistence.
- Being prepared.
- Maintaining communications.
- Believable integrity.

It's up to you to find the activities that work. Pound the pavements. Use shoe leather. Take samples and demonstrate your product. Get immediate feedback on what's wrong -- and what's right -- with the product.

What Doesn't Work In Sales

Don't try to persuade prospects to buy what they don't want. Selling requires more awareness and less pushy bravado. It requires more intelligence, versus blind coercive force.

Questions That Need to be Answered

You must answer these questions as you establish a business:

- What to sell?
- To whom to sell?
- Where to sell?
- When to sell?
- How to sell?

During a sales discussion, the following questions are in a salesperson's mind:

- How can I get the customer's attention?
- How can I hold his interest?
- Can I make enough on this sale?
- How can I get him to say "yes"?

Qualities Of An Effective Seller:

- Good listener
- Honest
- Persistent
- Creative
- Respectful

Good sellers are good listeners. Listening helps you to perceive the customer's needs, to discover what they are looking for. This helps the customer feel more connected to you.

Sellers can strengthen the tentacles of connection by demonstrating the following qualities:

- You believe in your ideas and in your product and have faith in yourself.
- You are forthright and don't beat around the bush.
- You are patient.
- You are open, collaborative, flexible, and a problem solver.
- You respect the customer's intelligence and right to make his/her own decisions.
- You show respect for your competition.
- You state your selling points and wait for questions.

Selling Conditions

If demand is greater than supply, ensure a smooth flow of your products.

If supply is greater than demand, focus on product improvement to increase demand.

Advertising

Definition
Advertising: drawing attention in a public medium to promote sales or attendance.

Effective advertising copy:

- Grabs your reader's attention
- Promises credible benefit
- Keeps the reader's interest
- Persuades your reader to take action.

However wonderful your product, your customer must determine he/she will gain value before parting with hard-earned money.

The questions in a customer's mind are:

"What can you do for me?"
"How can you help me?"
Your advertising must answer the questions.

The more often you repeat your ad, the more people will recognize your name and product.

In ads it is acceptable -- even required -- to use sentence fragments and "delightful non-words."

Your first sentence should be short -- no more than five words. Visual words attract customers because they create an image in the mind.

In direct mail, these ten words draw attention:

Free	New
You	Now
Win	Easy
Introducing	Today
Save	Guarantee

The Law of Business Survival

You need to make or create connections.

If you can't make a connection, it doesn't matter how beautiful the song, how masterful the book or how brilliant the invention -- the business fails.

Connections that promote, nurture, and sustain relationships turn your creation into a BUSINESS.

Definitions of Terms

Sales   Stores do it.

Selling   Insurance companies do it.

Marketing   Soap companies do it.

Connections   Successful startups do it.

A connection is like a tentacle. It can be of infinite variety and shape. It is anything that builds a bridge.

Examples Of Creating Connection

Example one:

An engineer needed a current sensor for an electric car control circuit. None were available on the market. To solve the problem, he created the necessary control devices.

First connection-

The circuit designer knew exactly what engineers needed -- he made a connection.

Second connection-

A small ad placed in a trade journal resulted in immediate sales.

Since then, his company sold over 8 million dollars worth of sensors. It's a niche market -- but highly profitable.

Third connection-

A website gives engineers all the required design information -- and includes a current sensor handbook. Result: Over 100,000 handbooks have been downloaded.

Example two:

You compose the next great musical hit. You send it to a publisher where it is filed with thousands of other submissions.

Or

You create the connection by playing your guitar for appreciative fans.

Feed the Hungers

You achieve connection by satisfying the wants and hungers of the public for participation, recognition, and/ or respect.

When launching a new product or finalizing an invention, the entrepreneur can build bridges by satisfying people's longings.

Connection solidifies when you exchange money to satisfy these yearnings. A performer connects by selling tickets and feeding the audience's hunger to participate.

The songwriter connects by having a performer sing his songs.

The sports entertainment industry exists to satisfy the public's desire for participation. The ticket is the connection.

Fashions exist to feed the public's desire for recognition. Awards ceremonies are examples of multiple connections. They feed the public's hunger for recognition, respect, and participation.

You can make connections at business breakfasts, lunches, and dinners. You can create opportunities by imagining what it's like to walk in other people's shoes. Search for basic yearnings. Apply your sensitivities to problems requiring your unique talents and experience.

Keep track of the number of new people you meet each week, the number of business cards you collect, and how many acquaintances you've greeted. Offer to have coffee with a person who emailed you looking for a job. (When he gets a job, he'll remember you as the one who cared.)

Customer Search

Once your product is available, the crucial element is connection.

You must identify customers. This effort is a far cry from the world of engineering and product development, which have a degree of predictability.

Customers may be hidden in a fog -- it may require considerable skill for you to send your product message out to the right audience. You have to explore the fog.

Some products like Apple devices are simply better mousetraps. People rush to buy Apple products because of their visibility, reputation and usefulness.

Finding Acceptance

Entrepreneurs create businesses AND push them to endure. Rejection strikes many business owners. Your strength and vision as a business founder keeps the flame alive until the market accepts your product.

For many creative people, it is often easy to conceptualize and create the invention, and/or to write a song or a book. It is more difficult to persuade the world to notice the VALUE of their creativity.

"I'll invent it and someone else can market it."
"I'll write the songs. Then I will find a publisher."

These thoughts lead to great frustration for creative people who crave recognition and commercial success.

The loneliness of the creative process is more suitable to inward-directed people. "Making the connection" is often beyond their natural strengths. In order to succeed, they need to beg, borrow, or steal methods of connection.

Most companies are compartmentalized. Engineering, production, and sales departments seldom cross-communicate. Not many know what marketing is – or what it does.

The difference in PROFIT companies is that the law of survival is integral to all phases of creation and development.

In many companies, "sales" or "marketing" implies it is someone else's responsibility. This interrupts the organic efforts required to develop projects. Consequently, new products often flop.

Create connections and success will follow.

"Building awareness is extremely important in industrial marketing because a prospect may not agree readily to see a salesperson representing an unknown company or product."
Barron's Marketing Dictionary

The Gallery of Innovation

Examples of producing WHAT to sell

These businesses existed long before the formulation of the Three Pillars of Business Success.

This table illustrates how The Three Pillars grades these ventures on their business health:

	Awareness	Solution	Connection
Yoga Radiance	A	A	C
Children Reading	A	C	D
Newverter	D	A	D
The Magic of Massage	A	A	C
Current Sensor	A	A	A
The Element Group	B	A	D
Venture Capital	A	A	A
SEE	C	C	D

Yoga Radiance

Inspiration: The beauty of Yoga poses.

Learn from Southern California's master yoga teachers as they guide you through four seasons of renewal. A dynamic series of Vinyasa flow yoga postures will take you to a new level. From the spring warm-up to the winter closing sequence, you'll invigorate your body, mind, and spirit with the power and grace of Yoga Radiance.

Discover the energy and youthful glow you deserve. This DVD includes a special restorative Lunar flow, a gentle evening series to prepare you for deep restful sleep.

Children Reading

Inspiration: Children learning to read.

To create reading experiences for preschoolers through their TV watching experiences. The fairy tale stories are recorded in book-like form on DVDs that the whole family can enjoy.

Newverter

Inspiration: Job survival.

Develop an inverter with semiconductor switches that produces precision three-phase sine wave power. It must be significantly lighter in weight and more efficient than anything else available.

Plan: Use computer analysis to minimize transformer and filter weight.

Think and visualize an avenue through multiple paths to a desired solution.

Execution: After following the plan of action, a solution finally emerged from the subconscious. The result: a breakthrough in inverter design surpassing fifty years of previous inventions. After a quick demonstration, a $10 million Army feasibility contract validated the concept. Practical battle field and aircraft electric power systems followed.

The Magic of Massage

Inspiration: A dream.

A powerful and energizing dream revealed the healing power of massage. This gave the business founder the desire to create a film capturing the beauty and inspirational power of massage techniques.

While the founders had no Hollywood film experience, the energy of the dream moved them to hire a manager, director, models and a cameraman.

They rented a sound stage, created a story board and began filming. Editing and marketing followed.

The resulting film illustrated the beauty and health producing power of the magic of massage. They sold 12,000 videos.

The Element Group
Inspiration: Homes for more families.

Letters, Numbers and Shapes

Inspiration: The business founder's 4-year-old son.

The desire to survive and to create wealth inspired a mother to create a business based on entertaining and educating her son. Her thinking and emotional energy brought into reality an enterprise suiting her financial resources. The educational app "Letters, Numbers and Shapes" appeals to toddlers by being fun, educational, and entertaining.

This app is much in demand to help children develop their reading, comprehension, and spatial skills.

Best of all, the business owner's son enjoys "Letters, Numbers and Shapes" immensely.

Venture Capital

Inspiration: The creative power of finance.

Do you want to do more with your life?

Discover the mysterious ways finance fosters the creation of wealth – how it unlocks the gifts of the ether and begets products for people.

Finance empowers by giving substance to the creative impulse. The human spirit engenders visions. For each person, new views of reality constantly flow through the mind. The spirit searches for a proper alignment of substance, money, the path, and need to give body to a vision of reality. It is this alignment that satisfies the "more" that you wish to do, and enables the doing of "more" to multiply.

The Wish: Finance beneficial relationships that enable fruits of the ether to beget products for the people.

We create beneficial relationships.

SEE

Inspiration: Groups of words created by the subconscious were assembled into a book titled "I begin to see..." The plan was to see if sayings from the subconscious would resonate with people.

The book authors received much criticism from poets and rejection from bookstores. Yet some people do love the book – including a few teachers who use it in classrooms.

Summary

The information laid out in PROFIT helps you travel the roads of creativity and invention to gain business profits.

The Three Pillars of Business Success model is a convenient way to take a snapshot of your business health. Two other companion strategies also help management succeed: harnessing emotional energy and winning the battle.

PROFIT teaches multiplied awareness through these strategies.

Strategy for the Pillars:

- Awareness: be aware of what is happening.
- Solution: solve the problem.
- Connection: make the connection.

Strategy for harnessing energy:

- Allow rejection to sharpen your awareness.
- Allow fear to broaden your vision.
- Allow anger to unblock your creativity.

Strategy for winning the battle:

- Turn off your internal dialogue.
- Have no expectations.
- Take responsibility.
- Be a warrior. * *

These strategies promote accurate perception leading to correct thinking and appropriate business actions.

The PROFIT Method combines thought, emotion, and fighting ability into a unified force. This force creates the business warrior.

Multiplied awareness is the internal light that powers your enterprise and leads you to excellence.

With PROFIT you:

• Unlock business blocks.
• Improve perception accuracy.
• Overcome emotional snags.
• Maintain strategic discipline to overcome adversity.
• Transform thoughts into actions.
• Cultivate multiplied awareness.
• Facilitate continuous innovation.

 PROFIT creates powerful neuron connections that form business brainpower. Your mind develops the ability to achieve business goals when provided a systematic approach to insure error-free perception and effective responses to business adversities.

In business the questions are: Who can get things done? Who can achieve, endure and succeed? It's all about accomplishment. Figure out a way to make it work, no matter what. You have to be tough, you have to be willing to take lots of body blows. Looking for that grit factor. Grit results in an increased ability to learn more and adapt faster. You love your business for the challenge and adventure.

Your business begins with a dream -- a vision. Your success requires Awareness, Solution and Connection. When you build your Three Pillars and launch your business, your dream becomes reality. Now you can enjoy the profits.

Appendix 1

About Money and Management

Financing some companies is like pouring money into a leaky boat – when you stop bailing, the boat sinks. Other start-ups are like sailing on a watertight ship -- steady and accumulating wealth.

PROFIT concentrates on nurturing the start-up business by focusing on growth potential.
****

Present Value

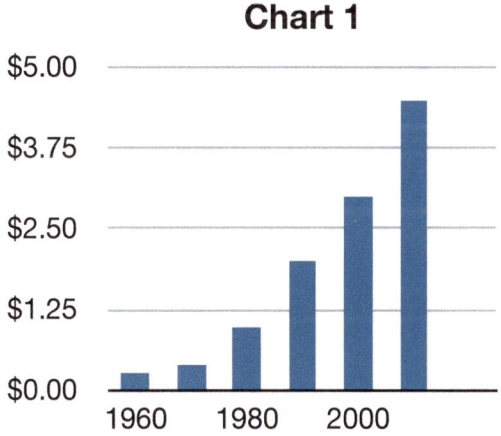

Chart 1

An 18 oz. box of corn flakes that cost $.27 in 1960 cost $4.50 in 2008; 16.7 times as much. Your 1960 dollar was worth 6 cents.

Caretaker Management vs Creative Management

Caretaker management resists change and believes the organization's future is predictable. Caretakers drive innovators out of the company. (Think of GM, Eastman Kodak, Westinghouse.) Caretakers do well in religious organizations and insurance companies, but are not compatible with high-tech companies and the military. Often,they show up in the wrong business. In competitive markets, businesses should be wary of the risks of caretaker management.

Creative management views change as necessary to survival. They believe the company's future is what they make of it. (Think Apple Computer, GE, Intel.)

Innovators with executive skills can sense the perils to the business and make adjustments. They use the Three Pillars to meet survival threats and to make changes. Seek management personnel who are constantly aware of what needs to be changed now -- and in the future. Creative managers pay attention to what is needed to survive.

Laws of Human Organization*

Law 1

In building an organization, you build on people who are "hangers-on."

Among a group of "hangers-on," you select those with patterns most similar to yours.

From those with the most similar patterns, you select people who have the most training.

Among those with the most training, you select the one who is the least creative.

Law 2

While building an organization, you prevent creative people from contributing because they could generate possibilities that do not benefit you.

Law 3

Keep salary and rewards at a level maximizing the "hanging-on" effect.

Law 4

Never make a decision: Allow events to take their natural course – then you will not be hung. Decisions threaten a rigid structure.

Law 5

Never make changes in your organization to make the structure less rigid.

Law 6

If you want to take over a program, organization or group, pick one in which all key individuals are dedicated to the activities of the program.

Stand outside and start giving subtle commands until you find a selection of prompts appealing to the group. When this happens, move in by rapidly increasing demands to swamp the group leadership. At the instant swamping occurs, dethrone the leader..

Group leadership methods of self-defense:

• Being aware of what is going on and pulling the usurper into the system

Or

- Seizing control of the input commands.

Or

- Desensitizing/buffering the system to input commands.

In your efforts to take control, use any strategy that maintains a comfortable level of unawareness within that group.

Law 7

In building your organization, distrust all those tied to the structure.

When key positions need to be filled, find someone from the outside. This guarantees discontinuity to any threatening forces developing in your organization.

Law 8

Control with threats and fear.

Law 9

Define responsibilities in vague terms, with generous amounts of overlap between individuals and departments.

Always place two individuals or departments in the same role.

This creates inner conflicts to prevent forces threatening your position. Keep these people and departments in a state of controlled conflict to sap their strength. Allow suspicion and distrust to exist on controlled levels.

Law 10

Ignore the information and directions from people in the lower echelons. Do not pay attention to complaints, criticisms, communication, cries, jokes, rumors, wishes, hopes, sincere feedback, and/or grumbling.

You can concentrate on the input from "favored" staff members. This makes planning and controlling easier. You and your core staff know what is happening and how to meet the flow of events impinging upon your organization.

Law 11

Operate on the principle that inventions and creative ideas generated by members of your organization belong to you, with no recognition or rewards required. Showering rewards on the working members of the organization takes away the spotlight from you.

Law 12

Organize your procedures, paperwork, methods, routines and operations by assuming every person in the organization is stupid. They are not creative, are unable to make decisions, and cannot assume responsibility beyond following the system's routines and rules.

Law 13

All life is the same
All thoughts are alike
Death is simply the absence of life.
Dead we cannot be because we are alive.

Law 14

The higher you rise in power and status, the

more threatened you will be by change. You will be more vulnerable to threats and losses. You will be frightened and will want more security.

Law 15

In a large population, there are people who wait for permission to do what they want. Hitler is an example. All that was required for his wishes to be carried out was that the population felt he had given them formal permission to do so.

Law 16

Those who want to control the actions of others are themselves relatively easy to control. Those who have very little desire to control others are much less "controllable" because they tend to be free spirits.

Law 17

In meetings of individuals with various levels of anxiety, the person with the most negative input will control the meeting. On impulse, the others will defend themselves against the attacker. Often, the most negative person will gain better control over the survival influences and factors that are controlling his life.

Law 18

Salesmanship: Take advantage of people's feelings of helplessness.

" The sales pitch sounds logical. If I buy the product I'll have the power to do something about my(appearance) (car) (health) (wealth). I can make my car run better."

Law 19

People want to believe they can be part of something good, just by being there or by spending a small amount of money. They feel like they deserve to have something good happen to them. (Examples: Elks clubs, gadgets, products that will make your car run better)

People are motivated to become distributors -- like promoters of TupperWare. They'll wait in long lines for World Series tickets and concert seats.

Law 20

"Most conflicts boil down to a control issue. Who is going to control who, with what."
Theodora Wells

Some Consequences

The laws of human organization apply -- without exception -- to industry, government, church bodies, and charitable institutions. Being aware of the laws helps you to deal successfully with organizations -- and to fulfill your needs.

For those who are creative, be forewarned by Law 1.

Law 1 means extremely talented or strong people do not fit into your organization and are "selected" out. Your organization cannot benefit from the input, strength, and diversity provided by people selected out.

For those who are out, they need to be aware of what is happening as early as possible, and choose one of these paths:

1. Start an organization of your own.
2. Find an organization you need to "hang-on" to and that accepts your patterns.
3. Stay with the ousted group and languish -- or change those in control.

Law 2 immobilizes the creative forces in your organization, and minimizes threats to the rigidity of your organization.

An organization built according to this law kills incentive, invalidates independent or creative thinking, and creates frustration.

When more determined individuals are creative, they pose a greater threat to your organization. You have to block them until their frustration forces them out completely.

Law 2 prevents organizations from becoming all-powerful. The process is self-limiting and – ultimately -- self-destructive. The manager has complete control of people in the structure – which creates the illusion of him/her controlling the organization.

In reality, key creative forces and true leaders have been in non-controlling positions. The organization begins to lack many vital characteristics -- like sensitivity to what is happening and the ability to see what is necessary to accomplish the organization's purposes.

Your goal as an organizer of the structure is rigidity. The sensitivity and force qualities must be kept in an impotent state for as long as possible, to preserve the rigidity of the human structure.

* These laws are not taught. They are inherent characteristics of human organizations. Knowledge of them can help the creative person understand what is going on in a company, minimizes mistakes as he/she achieves goals, and allows him/her to make more money.

Notable quote

"If there's a loophole, someone is going to drive a truck through it, and the people in the truck will get paid better than the people under it.
"Master the strange art of transforming nothing into something. See the world through an entrepreneur's eyes. Make yourself valuable.
"Modest skills collected in one person. That's how value is created"
"Failure is a process, not an obstacle". Move to where the action is. Distance is your enemy. Luck finds the doers. Learn the art of persuasion in all its forms.

Excerpt from "HowTo Get A Real Education" by Scott Adams, Wall Street Journal, April 9, 2011, Review Section.

Appendix II

The Warrior**

Carlos Castaneda taught about the mystical meaning of the warrior. One possible explanation -- in the experience of American culture -- is given here.

Turn Off The Internal Dialogue

Consider the shortstop in baseball -- eyes focused on the batter, body relaxed but alert, ready to respond in a fraction of a second to a ball streaking towards him at 100 miles per hour. He has a mental image of occupied bases and how many outs. He can't engage in his internal dialogue of problems, relationships, and future plans.

Have No Expectations

The ball can come at him as a line drive, ground ball, pop-up, or dribbler. How far to the left or right? There's no way to predict the outcome of a pitch. He doesn't guess. He responds.

Take Responsibility

His job is to catch the ball.

Be A Warrior

Make the out. He may be required to throw the runner out at first, to start a double play, or to throw the runner out at home. The warrior makes the out.

**Carlos Arana Castaneda] (anglicized from Castañeda; 25 December 1925 – 27 April 1998) was an American anthropologist and author.

www.ingramcontent.com/pod-product-compliance
Lightning Source LLC
Chambersburg PA
CBHW040812200526
45159CB00022B/500